The Highland Yarn Guide

Dwynwen Hopcroft

Loch Ness Knitting

Illustrations by Salina Jane

The Highland Yarn Guide

Copyright © 2019 Dwynwen Hopcroft

All rights reserved.

ISBN:9781698474298

DEDICATION

This book is dedicated to the wonderful and loyal customers of Loch Ness Knitting who have shown their passion and enthusiasm for every kind of Scottish Highland yarn.

The Highland Yarn Guide

The Highland Yarn Guide

CONTENTS

	Acknowledgments	i
1	Introduction	1
2	Frequently Asked Questions	4
3	Shopping Tips	11
4	Route 1	17
5	Route 2	27
6	Route 3	37
7	Route 4	47
8	Route 5	59
9	Route 6	69
10	Fleece to Finish Process	83

The Highland Yarn Guide

ACKNOWLEDGMENTS

Huge thank you to my husband Toby and talented artist Salina who were very patient listening to all the sheep and yarn facts.

The Highland Yarn Guide

1
INTRODUCTION

I run Loch Ness Knitting based in Drumnadrochit in the Scottish Highlands. Located on the shores of Loch Ness, Drumnadrochit village is one of the most popular places to visit in the Highlands and during the summer months of July and August can triple in population.

I'm fortunate that my location means I get to see so many of my customers face to face, and I love to hear about their journeys and reasons for visiting the Highlands. It also means I've been able to find out from them how difficult it has been to find authentic yarn (or any yarn) during their Highland adventures. One aim of this book is to assist with journey planning to help you make the most of a once in a lifetime trip.

Sadly, I've also met too many people who are disappointed that the expensive knitwear they bought locally was not made here in the Highlands, Scotland or even the UK, despite being sold as Scottish. During the busy summer months I'm asked every day where and how to find more authentic locally produced yarn and knitwear. This book is the answer to all those questions. Helping you to pro-actively show your customer support online or in person to a range of small businesses across the Scottish Highlands.

The wonderfully talented illustrator and knitter Salina Jane has provided illustrations full of life and character to help you spot some sheep breeds on your travels. She's also drawn the routes maps to give a sense of place, atmosphere and scale of the destinations included. You can find more of her work online at Saline Jane Art (www.salinajaneart.com).

I've also included a space for your own notes and journey planning. I often have customers arrive looking for yarn to match a specific project and we end up looking online for the exact details of how much yarn will be required. We often have to do a quick conversion yards and metres of yarn weight equivalents. Sometimes I'll also give advice about arranging colour combinations or making a pattern in a certain order to work frugally with the yarn amounts. So it's nice to have a space for project planning or simply keeping a track of your purchases.

The Highland Yarn Guide

2
FREQUENTLY ASKED QUESTIONS

1 I see lots of sheep, so where are all the yarn shops?

The sheep you see on your travels around Scotland are mainly for the food industry. In the 1960s the price of wool collapsed which led to farmers focusing on sheep breeds primarily for meat production. They are breeds that have been chosen for their ease of reproduction and lambing, producing mainly twins. They grow quickly into stocky and sturdy lambs that are then sold for meat. The fleece from their shearing is not of a good quality for yarn production, as it tends to have short, coarse and dense fibers. Where the quality is good enough to at least offset the costs of transportation, the fleece is bought by the farmers' cooperative organization British Wool (formerly known as the British Wool Marketing Board) and is mainly used for carpets and insulation.

There are some flocks of sheep in the Highlands that are correct breed for high quality fleece and fiber for wool. The farmers of these breeds usually have a direct relationship with a knitwear company or wool broker, such as Jamiesons of Shetland. This means that the Highland farmer is guaranteed a good, repeatable and reliable income for their high quality product. Unfortunately for hand knitters it means that this yarn is rarely available to smaller independent dyers.

The production process for manufactured knitwear in the Highlands, means that the yarn produced for this purpose is oiled and spun onto cones. You may find surplus and end cones for sale at some of the knitwear sites mentioned in this book.

Of course, there is also the production of various types of woven woollen fabric across the Highlands, such as Tweed and Tartan. Tweed fabric is a good match for the sturdy hard wearing fleece of Highland flocks located on the Outer Hebrides. This is not a book about weaving but there are a number of tweed and weave mills located along the routes in this book which provide interesting tours and will help to inform your overall understanding of the lifecycle of Highland yarn. If you are particularly interested in tartan then DC Dalgliesh is located further south in the Scottish Borders and is the only hand-crafted tartan mill in Scotland.

So, the fleece for the vast majority of the sheep you see on your travels in the Highlands is already spoken for, in fact in order to work directly with crofters the Mill or producer must apply for an Artisan exemption from British Wool. What is left for the indie dyer and hand knitter is a small section of the overall sheep farming market. This includes individual farms, crofts, small holders, rare breeds enthusiasts and island Community Interest Companies (CIC), who are not part of the British Wool organisation. These are the small businesses that I have tried to champion in this book. In my business, Loch Ness Knitting I aim to celebrate these as often as I can, however there is a limited amount of yarn available as the sheep are only sheared once or twice a year and the flocks are small.

The process to mill and transform fleece to fiber and yarn often requires large amounts of between 20kg to 500kg of scoured fleece. An adult sheep produces a fleece between 1-3kgs, which means that small flocks get blended together to make up the required total. At the time of writing crofters and farmers can expect to sell 1kg of fleece for between £0.60 to £0.90 (for fine breeds).

Finding a mill in the UK can also be a challenge as the collapse of the wool market during the 1960s led to the closure of many larger mills. Those that survived have struggled, but are finding a new market producing luxury textile goods, using Cashmere and other imported fibers.

Blending can also happen to improve the quality of yarn bringing together characteristics from each, for example the sturdiness of the Hebridean breed with the quality and sheen of the Blue Faced Leicester breed. Overall this means that pure single breed or single origin yarns in the Highlands are more difficult to produce and to find for sale.

In order to provide a consistent supply of high quality yarn for my business Loch Ness Knitting I choose to use the most reliable base of British Blue Faced Leicester from larger flocks located in Yorkshire and Cumbria, England, and Merino which is sustainably sourced from New Zealand.

2 Do you spin the wool yourself?

Most of the yarn on sale in the Scottish Highlands has been machine processed by mills around Scotland and England. There is some handspun yarn available, please recognize that this is an extremely skillful and special process that is not the norm for yarn in the

Scottish Highlands.

3 What is Scottish Cashmere?

Scottish Cashmere is a product where the base fiber, cashmere from goats, has been farmed elsewhere eg Mongolia or China, and imported to Scotland. Some or all of the final stages of production such as spinning, dyeing, weaving and knitting take place in Scotland.

4 What does Made in Scotland mean?

Items with this label information may have had all or none of their manufacturing take place in Scotland. It may mean the full process has taken place somewhere in Scotland or just the design. If you are aiming to support Scottish business please carefully question the shop you are buying from.

A similar confusion may arise when buying yarn that is not clearly labelled between the sheep breed and the origin of the fleece. Expert sheep breeders developed characteristics to suit the location of the flock as well as improve the quality of the animal. This was fairly localized and the resulting breed ended up becoming known by the location, eg Suffolk, Welsh, Hebridean, Dartmoor etc. A common misunderstanding that I explain regularly in the Loch Ness Knitting shop is that Shetland is a breed and a location. Not all Shetland sheep live on the island of Shetland, and not all sheep that live on the island of Shetland are Shetland sheep.

The term 'Native Shetland Wool' was granted Protected Designated Origin (PDO) in 2007. PDO's are granted under EU law to protect the unique heritage of traditional food and drink items, 'Native Shetland Wool' is the only wool item to have been granted this status.

This means the yarn and products bearing this specific term have been wholly produced on Shetland, following detailed stages as set out in the PDO application.

When I sell Shetland yarn I am generally referring to the breed, not the location, and I will clearly state the difference.

5 What does sustainable mean?

This term has **no legal definition**. Many people consider wool production to be inherently sustainable due to the renewable nature of the source, i.e. sheep, and the biodegradable nature of the fleece. However, for my business and the content of this book I use the term sustainable to refer to those businesses that are using a process that reduces waste, energy consumption and aims to eliminate wider ranging negative effects on the environment. This could mean reducing transport miles, improving packaging, changing energy suppliers.

6 Can I buy 10 of these?

Most of the Highland businesses included in this book are small independent family run, like my own. We generally don't hold large amounts of stock as supplies and storage are limited, see Question 1 above. It is not always economical for us to produce and hold large amounts of yarn for projects such as sweaters and blankets, unless they are custom orders. In my experience most customers are looking for one special skein or project to capture their holiday or yarn festival visit. That is not to say that sweater quantities are not available, but if you have a dream project in mind requiring a large amount of single matching dyelot yarn please get in touch in advance so that you are not disappointed. If this is not possible please talk to the vendor, we are experts in our products and can guide you towards patterns and techniques to work with multiple skeins.

The Highland Yarn Guide

3
SHOPPING TIPS

1 When you are planning your trip please check shop opening hours and be aware that some shops have different opening hours for peak Summer and off-peak Winter seasons.

2 If you would like to visit a croft or farm mentioned in this book please contact them in advance. Farm life is very busy and most will be happy to welcome you if you book in advance.
Off peak visits are generally better for more indepth conversations, July and August are peak season and likely to be very busy.

3 To meet multiple vendors in one hit please consider attending one of the yarn festivals mentioned. This will reduce your travel miles and many of them take place during off-peak Autumn/Winter providing valuable income for small businesses after the main tourist season has finished. Winter in the Scottish Highlands tends to be cold, dark and wet so it's not the time to enjoy a long road trip.

4 Be aware that many Highland dyers in this book are

running businesses from their homes. If I have not included their address it should be considered private. Please use their contact details to arrange sales.

5 If you are not able to visit in person please use this book to guide your online shopping in exploring and supporting authentic Scottish Highland yarn businesses.

Notes...

Notes...

Notes...

4
ROUTE 1:
A YARN TALE OF THREE CITIES

This route focuses on the East coast of Scotland, with picturesque fishing villages in Aberdeenshire, to industrial heritage in Dundee, before moving on to Perth and finishing with traditional life of the Highland croft in Newtonmore.

Harley of Scotland

44-46 Queen Street
Peterhead
Aberdeenshire
AB42 1TR

01779 472109

www.harleyofscotland.com

This family run knitwear business originally produced fisherman's stockings and later moved into knitwear inspired by the sweaters worn by the local fisherman. The factory is located on its original site, formerly herring fish yards. From Fair Isle sweaters to Herring Girl shawls, fishing heritage has an important part in the history of Scottish Highland yarn and knitwear making this a great place to begin your journey.

Harley's continues to produce traditionally inspired designs but now they have a zero waste process using tubular knitting machines. Some of the wool used is sourced locally from Shetland breed sheep, they also work with Italian wool and Scottish Cashmere (see Chapter 2).

Cookston Crafts

Ellon
Aberdeenshire
AB41 8DE

cookstoncrafts@hotmail.com

www.cookstoncrafts.com

Owner Claire set up Cookston Crafts in 2015 to share and celebrate her love of yarn and crafts. She has a bright and beautiful selection of luxury hand dyed yarns and crochet kits. Courses and events also take place regularly. Claire sells online and is a regular at many yarn festivals across Scotland.

Wool for Ewe

83-85 Rosemount Place
Aberdeen
AB25 2YE

01224 643738

info@woolforewe.com

www.woolforewe.com

A fabulous local yarn store (LYS) run by mother and daughter team Kathy and Faye. The store offers a mix of locally sourced and Scottish yarns as well as bigger brands. Wool for Ewe is also a great stop for picking up needles, notions and accessories.

A Yarn Tale

36A Thistle Street
Aberdeen
AB10 1XD

Ayarntale36@gmail.com

www.ayarntale.co.uk

A Yarn Tale is a lovely little LYS open Thursday to Sunday with an interesting selection of yarns put together by owner Kelly.

Bowfiddle Yarns

Durris
Aberdeenshire

info@bowfiddleyarns.com

www.bowfiddleyarns.com

Selling online and at yarn festivals Louise from Bowfiddle yarns is an indie dyer with a great eye for color. Her vibrant handdyed selection is inspired by the Scottish landscape and uses Merino and Alpaca from South America, and British Blue Faced Leicester.

Baa!

43 Evan Street
Stonehaven
Aberdeen
AB39 2ET

01569 668298

hello@baawool.co.uk

www.baawool.co.uk

Opening in 2018 this new LYS stocks a range of indie and artisan dyers curated by owner Janice. As an experienced designer and tutor Janice also offers a selection of skills workshops throughout the year. The shop is open from Wednesday to Saturday.

Murton Farm

Murton Trust
Murton Steading
Arbroath Road
Forfar
DD8 2RZ

01307 466041

murtontrust@murtontrust.org.uk

www.murtontrust.org.uk

The Murton Farm site has a lovely tea room, visitor farm and nature reserve. Book in advance for one of the rural skills days for an in depth look at weaving, hand spinning, fiber preparation and dyeing.

Fluph

fluphshop@gmail.com

www.fluph.co.uk

A small shop full of colourful gorgeous yarn and equally bright personality! Championing the yarn of local Dundee based indie dyer Rusty Ferret.

Perth Festival of Yarn

Perth

hello@perthfestivalofyarn.uk

www.perthfestivalofyarn.uk

This annual festival is conveniently located to attract both vendors and visitors from the Scottish Highlands and the Central Belt area. Check the website for dates and booking details.

Ewenique Fibres

Blairgowrie

www.eweniquefibres.etsy.com

A beautiful and bright selection of yarn and fibers on a variety of bases. Ewenique is a regular stand at yarn festivals.

Karelia House

Comrie Bridge
Aberfeldy
PH15 2LS

01887 822027

info@kareliahouse.co.uk

www.kareliahouse.co.uk

A medium sized yarn and craft store with a coffee shop. Stocking UK brand yarns, fabrics and patterns. Karelia House also offers courses and classes.

Highland Folk Museum

Kingussie Road
Newtonmore
PH20 1AY

01540 673551

Highland.folk@highlandhighlife.com

www.highlifehighland.com/highlandfolkmuseum

A showcase of historical traditional farm and crofting life in the Scottish Highlands. Occasional rural skills days with demonstrations in hand spinning and fiber preparation. Check the website in advance for opening hours and special events.

Moulin Yarns

Kinnaird farmhouse
Pitlochry
Perthshire
PH16 5JL

07756797411

davidw.kinnaird@btopenworld.com

www.moulinyarns.com

Moulin yarns is a small business with a wonderful back story of owner David being led astray in a knitting store by his wife Linda. They offer the most beautiful colourful selection of yarns and spinners will find a special welcome here. A focus on British yarns wherever possible.

Notes...

Notes...

Notes...

5
ROUTE 2:
SUN, SAND AND YARN

Starting in Inverness this route moves out to the stunning beaches of Nairn and would connect up beautifully with plans to walk the Moray Firth Costal Trail.

Kelpie Knits

Inverness

www.kelpieknits.com

Eilidh at Kelpie Knits is an indie dyer producing a delightful range of small batch hand dyed colours. Shop online or in person at one of our Highland yarn festivals.

Loch Ness Knit Fest

Inverness

01463 564013

www.lochnessknitfest.co.uk

This annual October yarn festival is based in Inverness, with a selection of classes and supporting social events, including boat tours on Loch Ness.

PurpleLinda Crafts

39 Firthview Drive
Inverness
IV3 8NS

contact@purplelindacrafts.co.uk

www.purplelindacrafts.co.uk

Owner Linda has a passion for crochet and sells a wide range of yarn and supplies in her mostly online store.

Nairn Wool Shop

6/6a Falconers Lane
Off High Street
Nairn
IV12 4DS

nairnwoolshop@yahoo.co.uk

www.nairnwoolshop.co.uk

A well-established LYS offering the main UK yarn brands. The shop also hosts groups and classes. Check the website for booking details.

Artisan Threads

Westwood
Littlemill
Nairn
IV12 5QL

07712045267

Info@artisanthreads.co.uk

www.artisanthreads.ecwid.com

Gill offers an open studio on Thursday from 10.30am to 6pm. She has a passion for local sourcing, hand spun yarn, textiles and weaving. This stop is a must for spinners!

Knockando Woolmill

Aberlour
Moray
AB38 7RP

01340 810345

office@kwc.co.uk

www.kwc.co.uk

Knockando mill is one of the highlights of this Highland grouping. The mill is a heritage project that has been set up by a charitable trust with a purpose to restore the site and equipment. The mill is currently producing small batches of yarn and woven cloth from locally sourced wool. Guided tours are available if booked in advance and check the website for seasonal opening hours.

Auld Mill Alpacas/ Alpaca Days Out/ Alpaca Farm Shop

Mossend Farm
Mosstowie
Elgin
Moray
IV30 8TU

07773968979

hello@alpacafarmshop.co.uk

www.alpacadaysout.co.uk

Whilst you can never have too many sheep in a book about Scottish Highland yarn it's nice to offer a little variety. How about an alpaca palette cleanser? This lovely little farm shop sells yarn, fleeces and finished items made from their alpaca herd. Advance booking is essential for the Alpaca Tours. Shop open from 10am to 1pm on Saturdays.

Johnstons of Elgin

Newmill
Elgin
IV30 4AF

01343 554099

customerenquiries@johnstonsofelgin.com

www.johnstonsofelgin.com

A medium to large manufacturer of luxury knitwear. Johnstons uses a range of fibers; their Cashmere is sourced from herds in Mongolia, China and Afghanistan. They also use Australian Merino, South American Alpaca and cotton from Central America (Belize). The raw fiber is transported to Scotland where it is processed, dyed and made into finished garments. The family owned business employs over 1000 people, many of whom have been with them for over 20 years. The workers are highly skilled and many processes are hand finished. If you are buying luxury fibers as yarn or finished items, or thinking of buying them in the future a visit to Johnstons is a great way to inform your choices. Free mill tours are available by booking in advance.

Portsoy Wool Fest

Portsoy

Facebook page Wool @ Portsoy

This annual wool festival is a true highlight of the Highland yarn year. Started by the local knitters as a celebration of wool and fiber, and boost to the local economy. Held in August prepare yourself for the heat or downpour of the Scottish summer, most likely both! Enjoy the bustle of this unique event and remember to wear flat shoes for the walk between the different local venues.

Notes...

Notes...

Notes...

Notes...

BEN NEVIS
WEST HIGHLAND CRAFTS
ISLE OF MULL
ULVA
IONA WOOL
IONA PEBBLES
LAMBS WOOL
IONA
ISLE OF MULL WEAVERS
FERRIES
KILAVREE CROFT
THE WOOL AND NEEDLE CRAFT CENTRE
DYE
LYS
KILMARTIN MUSEUM
M
LOCH LOMOND & THE TROSSACHS NATIONAL PARK
GLASGOW

6
ROUTE 3:
BIG MOUNTAINS AND SMALL ISLANDS

This route explores the mountains, glens and small islands of the West Coast of Scotland. I rediscovered knitting when I was attending Stirling University, and Ravelry hadn't been invented yet. I had moved up to Scotland from Wales and needed an economical solution to the surprise that Scotland was far colder in real life than it had been in my imagination. I used to spend weekends exploring and hiking in this area so this route holds many special memories for me.

West Highland Crafts

Wendy Wilson
West Highland Crafts
12 Dal nam Mart
Strontian
Acharacle
PH36 4BB

www.westhighlandcrafts.co.uk

West Highland Crafts is a fabulous collaboration of local artisans and craft makers working in the Ardnamurchan area of the West Highlands. When makers live rurally it is often not practical to maintain a retail space as well as a home workshop. These collective efforts can be purchased online and in local markets they showcase the skill and creativity of these local Highland makers.

The Wool and Needlecraft Centre

13 Argyll Sq
Oban
PA34 4PG

01631 564469

info@woolandneedlecraftcentre.co.uk

www.woolandneedlecraftcentre.com

A lovely little yarn store mostly serving local knitters and crafters. This is a great stop for your needles and notions. The store also has a selection of Scottish wool from the New Lanarkshire Heritage project and the Crofters Blend project on Shetland. Closed on Sunday.

Kilmartin Museum

Kilmartin
Lochgilphead
Argyll
PA31 8RQ

01546 510278

admin@kilmartin.org

www.kilmartin.org

A fascinating museum giving a unique insight into ancient life in the Highlands. It is worth planning your trip to coincide with one of the guided walk events, which are led by volunteers at the museum.

Kilvaree Croft

Oban

Julia.hamilton@live.co.uk

www.kilvareecroft.com

Kilvaree is a working croft with its own flock of rare breed Soay sheep. Please contact the owners in advance if you would like to visit as croft life can be very busy. Products made from the Kilvaree felt are available to buy online or in the craft shop in Oban.

Isle of Mull Weavers

Ardalanish Farm
Bunessan
Isle of Mull
PA67 6DR

01681 700 265

info@ardalanish.com

www.ardalanish.com

A mixed farm with hardy Highland cows and Hebridean sheep. This is a must see visit, as it is one of the few places where they have a truly flock to finish process. This is due to the installation of a small mill which allows the farm to process its own fleece, and that of other farmers on the island. This local processing means a better deal for the island farmers involved as they do not have to pay transport costs to get the fleece to the mainland. The mill also works with smaller amounts of fleece which is a better fit for the croft sized flock. Yarn and fiber in the natural flock colours is available to buy online and in person. A selection of finished items is also available.

Iona Pebbles Arts and Crafts

Thistledo
Isle of Iona
PA76 6AP

01681 700 362

Val@ionapebbles.co.uk

www.ionapebbles.co.uk

Iona Pebbles is a small business selling a range of handmade craft items and their own brand of yarn. The yarn is 100% lambswool from their own flock of Scotch Mule and Texel sheep. The yarn processing takes place elsewhere in the UK. Shop online or in person Monday to Friday.

Iona Wool

Iona Craft Shop
Isle of Iona
Argyll
PA76 6SJ

01681 700 001

info@ionacraftshop.com

www.ionawool.com

This limited edition yarn is an authentic representation of modern Highland crofting life and yarn. To produce the yarn fleece is gathered from a number of mixed flocks on the island. The fleece is partially processed on the island and then sent to be milled elsewhere in the UK. Working in this collaborative way gives the best deal for these island farmers. The mixed breed yarn is available to buy online or in person and comes in natural breed colours. Finished knitwear is also available to buy.

AUTHOR NOTE...

Caledonian Wool

High Street
Fort William

www.thecaledonianwool.com

This yarn shop is due to open in November 2019 and was not open at the time of editing. The pre-opening information states that the shop intends to stock Scottish yarn, handspun wool and offer craft courses.

Notes...

Notes...

Notes...

Notes...

N
HARRIS
BIRLINN YARN CO.
VIRTUAL YARN
NORTH UIST
UIST WOOL
SOUTH UIST
HEBRIDEAN ISLES CO.
SHILASDAIR
THE HEBRIDEAN ALPACA CO.
SKYE
THE HANDSPINNER
HAVING FUN
SOAY
RUM
SMALL ISLES
TJFROG
INVERNESS
LOCH NESS KNIT FEST
LOCHNESS KNITTING
PURPLE LINDA CRAFTS
LOCH NESS SPINDLES
KELPIE KNITS
BUNLOIT WOOLERY
CAIRNGORMS NATIONAL PARK

7
ROUTE 4:
HIGHLANDS AND ISLANDS

This route starts in Inverness and then winds out to the stunning Isle of Skye before crossing by ferry over to the Outer Hebrides islands of Uist, Berenay, Harris and Lewis. Visiting Inverness, Loch Ness and Skye is one of the most popular routes for tourists, here I encourage you to take your time and be a little more adventurous by continuing on to my husbands homeland of the Outer Hebrides. This route showcases the breadth and beauty of the Scottish Highlands, from coast to Lochs, mountains and Machair.

Kelpie Knits

Inverness

www.kelpieknits.com

Small batch hand dyed yarn from this Highland based indie dyer. A regular at yarn festivals.

Loch Ness Knit Fest

Enquries to
27 Tower Drive
Inverness

IV2 5FD

01463 564 013

www.lochnessknitfest.com

Inverness based festival taking place annually in October. A selection of classes and supporting events, including boat tours on Loch Ness. The marketplace includes demonstrations and a range of vendors.

PurpleLinda Crafts

39 Firthview Drive
Inverness
IV3 8NS

contact@purplelindacrafts.co.uk

www.purplelindacrafts.co.uk

Owner Linda has a passion for crochet and sells a wide range of yarn and supplies in her mostly online store.

Loch Ness Knitting

Taigh Anns A'Choille
Kilmore Road
Drumnadrochit
IV63 6TS

01456 450 472

lochnessknitting@gmail.com

www.lochnessknitting.com

Naturally dyed yarn using sustainable materials gathered from the local Loch Ness Cafes and woodlands. Yarn is sustainably sourced New Zealand Merino – non-mulesing, British Blue Faced Leicester and a Yarn of the Month celebrating Scottish and British Rare Breeds. Hand dyed yarn, handmade items, patterns, courses and demonstrations available. Shop hours Tuesday to Saturday 10am to 6pm.

Bunloit Woolery

3 Balbeg
Bunloit
IV63 6XQ

01456 450 301

bunloitwoolery@btinternet.com

A small croft business near Loch Ness. Bunloit have their own flock of Gotland and Gotland/Shetland cross sheep. They sell fleece, locks and batts, and some handspun yarn. Spinning courses are also available throughout the year and they regularly attend yarn festivals.

Loch Ness Spindles

Drumnadrochit

info@lochnessspindle.co.uk

www.lochnessspindle.co.uk

Loch Ness Spindle is a dealer for Schacht spinning wheels, weaving looms and accessories in the UK. They carry a stock of Schacht Ladybug, Sidekick and Matchless spinning wheels. Please contact Olga in advance if you are hoping to visit in person.

TJ Frog

Aird of Sleat

Isle of Skye

www.tjfrog.co.uk

Online shop and regular yarn festival stallholder. Specialist maker of Dorset buttons. TJ Frog are also offering their own brand of yarn blending British Poll Dorset and Hebridean wool from the Isle of Skye.

The Handspinner Having Fun

Old Pier Road
Broadford
Isle of Skye
IV49 9AE

01471 822 476

bev@handspinnerhavingfun.com

www.handspinnerhavingfun.com

Bev offers a fantastic colourful selection of yarns and finished items with a commitment to sourcing local and Scottish where possible. Hand spun and hand dyed yarn and fiber available. Workshops also available throughout the year.

The Hebridean Alpaca Company

1 Lochside
Dunvegan
Isle of Skye
IV55 8WB

hebrideanalpacas@sky.com

www.hebridean-alpacas.co.uk

This is a lovely boutique shop selling yarn and accessories from the Isle of Skye's own herd of Alpacas. The shop is located alongside other makers and is a hub of local artisan and craft work.

Hebridean Isles Trading Company – Isle at the Edge

Eilean Or
1A Edibane
Portree
Isle of Skye
IV51 9PR

01470 582 261

yasmin@island-at-the-edge.co.uk

www.island-at-the-edge.co.uk

Yarn and finished items from Hebridean, Black Cheviot and North Ronaldsay sheep grazing on Skye. Traditional Gansey knitting to order and courses throughout the year. Shop online or in person and choose between mill or handspun yarn from their own croft flock.

Shilasdair

Shilasdair Yarn
Culnacnoc
Portree
Isle of Skye
IV51 9JH

01470 562 248

hello@shilashair-yarns.com

www.shilasdair-yarns.com

A much loved and well established yarn business, now under new ownership and with new premises. Still passionate about yarn and natural dyeing. Own brand yarn for sale uses British Blue Faced Leicester (BFL) and Shetland breed sheep. Also, a DK Wensleydale and Aran weight blended BFL. Spun in the UK and dyed at the Shilasdair workshop. Yarn is naturally dyed using a variety of locally sourced materials and some imported traditional materials such as indigo and madder.

Uist Wool

The Mill and Wool Centre
Scotvein
Grimsay
Isle of North Uist
Outer Hebrides
HS6 5JA

01870 602 597

www.uistwool.com

Spinning mill and wool centre selling own brand yarn. This mill works with local farmers and crofters to locally source fiber. Hebridean based flocks have a reputation for rustic and coarse wool that is out of favour with most hand knitters. Traditionally this type of yarn was a good fit for the requirements of sturdy outdoor garments with some level of water resistance. Modern living has changed tastes to finer lighter yarns. Having a fleece to finish relationship through local sourcing Uist Wool is continually working to improve the quality of fiber and yarn to produce a premium product worthy of this stunning location.

Birlinn Yarn Company

Sunhill
Isle of Berneray
Outer Hebrides
HS6 5BQ

01876 540 283

meg@birlinnyarn.co.uk

www.birlinnyarn.co.uk

Small batches of yarn from Hebridean sheep raised in a sustainable way of the Isle of Berneray. Yarn available to buy online or in person at Puffin Studio Crafts, The Old Post Office, Creagorry, Benbecula.
Monday to Saturday 10.30 -16.30
The croft is happy to welcome visitors by appointment between April and September. Please arrange this with them in advance.

Virtual Yarns

42 Gress
Isle of Lewis
Eilean Siar
HS2 0NB

info@virtualyarns.com

www.virtualyarns.com

Online only shop from the family run business of knitwear designers Alice and Jade Starmore. Specialists in traditional knitting designs. Yarn, patterns and finished garments available.

Notes...

Notes...

Notes...

Notes...

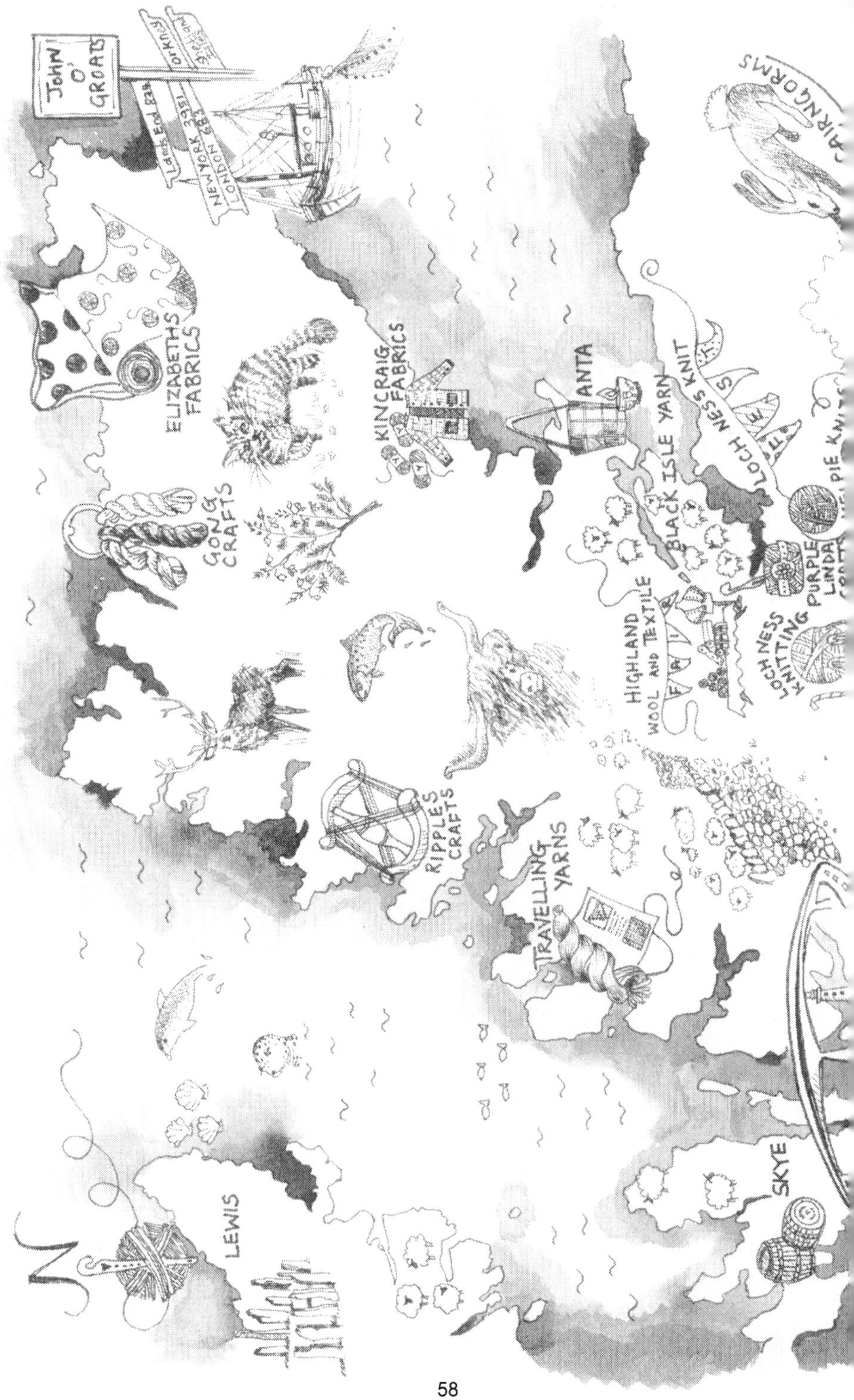

JOHN O' GROATS
ELIZABETHS FABRICS
GONG CRAFTS
KINCRAIG FABRICS
ANTA
BLACK ISLE YARN
LOCH NESS KNIT
HIGHLAND WOOL AND TEXTILE
LOCH NESS KNITTING
RIPPLES CRAFTS
TRAVELLING YARNS
LEWIS
SKYE

8
ROUTE 5:
NORTH COAST 500

For those planning a journey along the popular North Coast 500 (NC500) driving route this is a handy list of yarn stops along the way. The NC500 route was launched in 2015 and has proven extremely popular, with a dramatic increase in visitor numbers for the Highland towns and villages along the way. Prior to the establishment of the route many of the yarn businesses in the Highlands traded exclusively online or at yarn festivals. As a result of NC500 success business arrangements are changing, and some local funding has been allocated to assist with development. One of the most welcome changes is the revival of local markets featuring produce, craft and art. Unfortunately, there is no main list of market times and locations, if you would like to time your visit to coincide with one of these I suggest you contact Visit Scotland for further assistance. Overall this route is one to watch for fresh yarn possibilities.

Kelpie Knits

Inverness

www.kelpieknits.com

Small batch hand dyed yarn from this Highland based indie dyer. A regular at Highland yarn festivals.

Loch Ness Knit Fest

Enquiries to
27 Tower Drive
Inverness
IV2 5FD

01463 564 013

www.lochnessknitfest.com

Inverness based festival taking place annually in October. A selection of classes and supporting events, including boat tours on Loch Ness. The marketplace includes demonstrations and a range of vendors.

PurpleLinda Crafts

39 Firthview Drive
Inverness
IV3 8NS

contact@purplelindacrafts.co.uk

www.purplelindacrafts.co.uk

Owner Linda has a passion for crochet and sells a wide range of yarn and supplies in her online store.

Loch Ness Knitting

Taigh Anns A'Choille
Kilmore Road
Drumnadrochit

IV63 6TS

01456 450 472

lochnessknitting@gmail.com

www.lochnessknitting.com

Naturally dyed yarn using sustainable materials gathered from the local Loch Ness Cafes and woodlands. Yarn is sustainably sourced New Zealand Merino – non-mulesing, British Blue Faced Leicester and a Yarn of the Month celebrating Scottish and British Rare Breeds. Hand dyed yarn, handmade items, patterns, courses and demonstrations available. Shop hours Tuesday to Saturday 10am to 6pm.

Highland Wool and Textiles Fair/ Highland Wool Fest

01381 610 301

info@highlandwoolandtextiles

Facebook Page Highland Wool and Textiles

Annual Highland Wool Festival taking place in Dingwall, usually in May. The organizers also arrange a smaller de-stash event taking place in Autumn. This lovely event features many local yarn, fleece and fiber businesses and has a great location full of atmosphere in the Dingwall market.

Travelling Yarns

Poolewe

07730850866

info@travellingyarns.com

www.travellingyarns.com

Mobile yarn shop often found at craft fairs, markets and wool shows. Also available to buy online.

Ripplescrafts

124 Clachtoll
Near Lochlnver
IV27 4JD

www.ripplescrafts.com

A beautiful selection of yarn hand dyed by Helen in a variety of weights and colours, available to buy online or in person. Helen's yarn inspiration comes from the breathtaking scenery of her Assynt surroundings and her workshop is a convenient stop on the NC500 route.

Gong Crafts

12 Lotts Way
Skerray
KW14 7TH

01641 521 764

contact@gongcrafts.scot

www.gongcrafts.scot

A small business focusing on botanical dyeing onto British sourced yarn. Fibre and handspun also available.

Elizabeths Fabrics

1-3 Brabster Street
Thurso
Caithness

KW14 7AP

01847 896 497

shop@elizabethsfabrics.co.uk

www.elizabethsfabrics.co.uk

A small multi-craft shop selling main brand yarn.

Ashcroft Makers

Rogart

IV28 3XE

01408 698 248

contact@ashcroftmakers.com

www.ashcroftmakers.com

A small indie yarn business run by Finn selling hand dyed yarn and hand made knitted items.

Notes...

Notes...

Notes...

Notes...

N
AA
HELLY
UP
JAMIESONS OF SCOTLAND
URADALE FARM
JAMIESON & SMITH
SHETLAND WOOL WEEK
ANDERSON AND CO.
FAIR ISLE
ORKNEY WOOL
WOOLSHED
NORTH RONALDSAY YARN
ORKNEY ANGORA
QUERNSTONE KNITWEAR
A YARN
ORKNEY TWEED
LITTLE ORKNEY DYE SHED
HILARY GRANT
JUDITH GLUE

9
ROUTE 6:
VIKING TRAILS

The big adventure route for enjoying boats, planes and sheep! Strictly speaking Orkney and Shetland are not part of the Highlands, administratively or geographically. They lie off the mainland of Scotland and are part of a group containing over 100 islands that are sometimes referred to as the 'Northern Isles'. The remote location does not automatically mean isolation, these islands have been populated since Neolithic times, although only became part of Scotland in 1472. There is good grazing, excellent fishing and more recently employment in oil and increasing tourism. This route is one for the seasoned traveler as it requires coordination across modes of transportation and the ability to cope with potential cancellations. The ferry and plane transfers can experience poor weather at any time of year.

Also, be aware of UK daylight savings time, on the last Sunday on October clocks in the UK go back by 1 hour, meaning shorter days during the Autumn and Winter months. For locations in the Highlands, the Outer Hebrides and the Northern Isles this has a more extreme effect than other parts of the UK. During the Winter we have fewer hours of daylight, as little as five and a half hours on the most northern isle, a precious resource for outdoor workers like farmers.

The Quernstone Knitwear

41 Victoria Street
Stromness
Orkney
KW16 3BS

01856 852 900

info@quernstone.co.uk

www.quernstone.co.uk

A beautiful range of knitwear made using UK yarns. Items are made by hand and machine knitting by home based knitters across the islands. The shop also has some yarn from the Little Orkney Dye Shed if you haven't got time to visit Pam in Steness.

Orkney Wool

Burnside
Settiscarth
Orkney
KW17 2PA

orkneywool@runbox.com

www.orkneywool.com

A small business selling a special blend of Texel breed yarn raised on Orkney. This fleece is spun and dyed by the Natural Fibre Company, based in Cornwall (www.thenaturalfibre.co.uk) The yarn is also available to buy in Kathy's Knits, Edinburgh (www.kathysknits.co.uk).

PS *If you're stopping in Edinburgh pop your head into the Ginger Twist Studio for more awesome hand dyed loveliness.*

The Little Orkney Dye Shed

Button
Steness
Orkney
KW16 3HA

01856 851 169

pam@littleorkneydyeshed.co.uk

www.littleorkneydyeshed.co.uk

A colourful little business that welcomes visitors from Tuesday to Friday 2-4pm from April to September. A great stop for knitters, crochet fans, spinners and felters. The yarn base is North Ronaldsay and is dyed using a selection of bright acid dye colours.

Judith Glue

Inverness and Orkney

www.judithglue.co.uk

A boutique shop selling Judith's Orkney knitwear designs. Knitwear is made on Orkney using a group of 6 knitters. Designs are made from Scottish lambswool and Italian Merino.

Hilary Grant

Houth
Houton
Orphir
Orkney Islands
KW17 2RD

info@hilarygrant.co.uk

www.hilarygrant.co.uk

Modern Scottish knitwear design from Hilary and the gang at this small independent studio. Finished items are designed on Orkney and then made using yarn that is spun and dyed in the Scottish Borders.

Woolshed

The Woolshed
Benlaw
Costa
Evie
Orkney
KW17 2NN

01856 751 305

thewoolshed@btinternet.com

www.woolshed-orkney.co.uk

Specialists in using rare breed North Ronaldsay seaweed eating sheep. The shop sells fleece, knitwear, yarn and a range of handmade accessories.

A Yarn

45 Albert Street
Kirkwall
KW15 1HQ

01856 870 818

annieglue@aol.com

www.annieglue.com

A small shop specializing in knitwear sales and local gifts.

Orkney Tweed

Grindigar
Deerness
Orkney
KW17 2QJ

01856 741 777

nancy@orkneytweed.co.uk

www.orkneytweed.co.uk

A selection of accessories from a local Zwartbles sheep flock. Fleece is processed at the local mini mill on North Ronaldsay and then finished on Shetland at the Jamiesons mill.

Orkney Angora

Isle of Sanday
KW17 2AZ

01857 600 421

info@orkneyangora.co.uk

www.orkneyangora.co.uk

A small family business run by former Angora farmers. Spun Angora is imported from China for washing, dyeing and winding, The business is entirely open about its sourcing and aims for the highest animal welfare standards in its suppliers.

North Ronaldsay Yarn

Sangar
North Ronaldsay

KW17 2BG

01857 633 297

www.northronaldsayyarn.co.uk

A community owned business with the entire wool process based on the island. From fleece to fiber and finished yarn, in natural colours from the famous seaweed eating sheep. Finished knitwear is also available.

Shetland Wool Week

Shetland Museum and Archives
Hay's Dock
Lerwick
Shetland
ZE1 0WP

info@shetlandwoolweek.co.uk

www.shetlandwoolweek.com

A world famous, well-established and week long festival of Shetland wool and yarn. Often featuring famous guest teachers and tutors from around the world. A visit to Shetland Wool Week is at the top of most knitting wish lists.

Shetland Knitwear

Anderson and Co
60-62 Commercial Street
Lerwick
Shetland
ZE1 0BD

01595 693 714

enquries@shetlandknitwear.com

www.shetlandknitwear.com

Look for the Shetland Lady symbol to support authentically Shetland produced garments at this knitwear outlet.

Jamieson and Smith

90 North Road
Shetland
ZE1 0PQ

01595 693 579

mailroom@shetlandwoolbrokers.co.uk

www.shetlandwoolbrokers.co.uk

If you've been researching a trip to Shetland for yarn then you'll probably have seen photos of the amazing selection of yarn and colours on offer from Jamieson and Smith. 80% of the wool produced on Shetland is purchased by Jamieson and Smith. They purchase from around 700 Shetland based crofters and farmers. Now owned by Curtis Wool Direct based in Yorkshire.

Uradale Farm

East Voe
Scalloway
Shetland
ZE1 0US

01595 880689

www.uradale.com

Shetland Organics Community Interest Company was set up to support and promote the organic production of sheep and cattle across Shetland. They deserve a special mention for their work to achieve the special status of Protected Designated Origin (PDO) for the term 'Native Shetland Wool'. Uradale Farm is one of the success stories from this dedication and hard work to produce organic Shetland produce. It's a journey that started back in 2001 and is now showing the most beautiful yarn results as 'Native Shetland Wool'. The Uradale yarn is recreation of heritage yarns both in durability and some rustic hand feel. They sell a range of natural fleece colours and organically dyed colours. The yarn has inspired Trollenwol designers Marja de Haan, Anne de Haan and Hilly van der Sluis, and features in several of the patterns in their book *Shetlandic Knitting*.

Jamiesons of Shetland

Sandness Industrial Estate
Sandness
Shetland
ZE2 9PL

lerwick@jamiesonsofshetland.co.uk

www.jamiesonsofshetland.co.uk

A family owned business dating back to the 1890's. Their own brand of Jamiesons yarn using the Shetland breed is perfectly matched to traditional styles of stranded and lace knitting.

Notes...

Notes...

Notes...

Notes...

Notes...

The Highland Yarn Guide

10
FLEECE TO FINISH PROCESS

Understanding the journey from fleece to finished knit, information provided by British Wool (www.britishwool.org.uk) and the Campaign for Wool (www.campaignforwool.org).

Shearing

Usually done at least once or twice a year, between April and June. The fleece is cut by hand, using electrical shears, from each sheep. The sheep are sheared one at a time and it is a special skill, an experienced shearer can process 900 ewes in one day, taking around 2 minutes per ewe. Farmers employ gangs of specialist shearers to work fast and process the flock with minimum distress.

Farmers also chose the warmest and driest time of year as the fleece takes up to 6 weeks to regrow, providing insulation and protection for the sheep as they go into the Autumn and Winter season.

Without shearing most breeds of sheep will not shed their fleece and it will quickly become hot, uncomfortable, matted and maggot infested.

At this point fleece going on to the British Wool system is sewn into bags.

Grading and Auction

Fleece continuing through the British Wool system will be graded for quality. The graded fleece is then auctioned.

Scouring

The mill, manufacturer, crofter or artisan then begins the process of working with the fleece to transform it into yarn and cloth.

Scouring is a process of washing the field muck, mud and sheep droppings from the fleece. Traditionally fleece were scoured in local rivers where the flow of water would help to lift and carry the dirt downstream away from the fleece. Water in Scotland is considered to be naturally beneficial for washing fleece as it is soft, i.e. does not tend to contain dissolved minerals such as calcium and magnesium which would make the fiber brittle and prone to breaking in the subsequent processing. Although some soap helps the process nowadays, agitation is minimal as it runs the risk of felting the fleece.

Carding

Fleece is carded by machine or hand to lay the fibers of the fleece in the same direction. This process removes the worst knots and tangles from the fleece, which is now recognizable as fiber.

Combing

Machines then comb the fiber gently releasing the natural curls and kinks that occur in the fleece. Combing by hand or machine gives a beautiful smooth finish to the fiber in preparation for spinning.

Spinning

The fleece is now recognizable as clean, soft fiber that can be spun by hand, or more often by machine. Long sturdy fibers are easier in both processes, reducing breakage and fluff gathering in the machines. The process of twisting fibers together to make yarn is centuries old, the Inverness Museum and Art Gallery has a fine collection of spindles, also known as a whorl or dealgan.

Dyeing

Dyeing can take place before or after the knitting and weaving process. The application color, from natural or artificial pigments, to the protein based wool fibers.

Knitting and Weaving

The transformation of yarn into cloth or garments, both processes can be carried out by hand or machine and are distinctly different in the results.

Fulling or Waulking

This process is often shown in historical films and dramas with scenes portraying Highland life. Although if televisions had smell then it would probably be far less popular or intriguing. Fulling, also known in the Highlands as Waulking, is a secondary process of cleaning and agitation, and takes place after cloth has been woven (or knitted). The cleaning was carried out by the application of stale urine, which is naturally rich in ammonia. The agitation by human (usually female) hands or feet then took place, Highlanders would often sing as they worked, creating the oral tradition of waulking songs.

The result of waulking was a thickened cloth of matted woolen fibers. The cloth required further manipulation by stretching on tenterhooks, to ensure an even finish. It was a long and labour intensive process but the result was known to be sturdy, soft and waterproof cloth.

Fulling continues to be an important part of the textile finishing process for woven wool cloth, but is no longer using human urine in the Highlands. Today alkaline or ammonia soaps are a reliable substitution, and the finished cloth is sometimes referred to as boiled wool.

ABOUT THE AUTHOR

Dwynwen Hopcroft is the owner of Loch Ness Knitting and the author of two other books, My Colourful Kitchen and My Colourful Garden. Dwynwen is passionate about sustainability and working with respect to the beautiful Highland landscape that surrounds her location in Drumnadrochit. As well as being an innovative sustainable natural dyer Dwynwen is a knitwear designer, with patterns and finished items for sale online and in person. Occasionally Dwynwen consults and contributes to large collaborative art and textiles projects, more information on this and all her work can be found at www.lochnessknitting.com

Printed in Great Britain
by Amazon